Daddy,
Where are you!

Michele Sweeney

Foreword by Pastor Richard T. Stonewall, Sr.

Daddy, Where Are You!
By: Michele Elmira Sweeney

Foreword by: **Pastor Richard T. Stonewall, Sr.**
Cover Design By: Jazzy Kitty Publishing
Cover Photograph by: http://www.simplifiedbee.com/2012/09/adorable-kids-bedroom-designer-house-ruby.html

Logo Designs By: Andre M. Saunders
Editor: Anelda L. Attaway
Co-Editor: Michele Sweeney
Photographs By: First Lady Kimberly Thomas, Michele Sweeney (The Late William F. Sweeney Jr.), simplifiedbee.com

© 2013 Michele Sweeney
ISBN 978-0-9851453-7-8
Library of Congress Control Number: 2013901970

All rights reserved. This book is protected under the copyright laws of the United States of America. This book may not be copied or reprinted for commercial gain or profit. The use of short quotations or occasional page copying for personal or group study is permitted and encouraged. Permission will be granted upon request. For Worldwide Distribution. Printed in the United States of America Published by Jazzy Kitty Greetings Marketing & Publishing, LLC. Utilizing Microsoft Publishing Software. The names in this book have been changed to protect their identity.

This book is especially dedicated to Turquoise Trowery, Jeremy Trowery, Pedro Donato Jr., Dorian Pennington Jr., and Rayhan Perry - My 5 beautiful children.

I want you all to know that through all of my challenges and my hard times that I never regretted ever having any one of you. You will always be the greatest accomplishment in my life. Everything in life happens for a reason and I know that God has allowed me to birth five wonderful children who all have very different gifts and talents. And for whatever the reason he allowed you all to be born to me, three I raised and two I did not; but even in that he allowed it, and I love you all.

William F. Sweeney Jr., "Daddy"

A special thank you to my deceased father, William F. Sweeney Jr., who made it possible for me to write this book. He gave me life. May you rest in peace "Daddy", and know that I wish so much that you could have been here to see this day and God's handiwork being done. You continue to sleep until the day that the trumpet sounds and I am able to be caught up with you and see your face and let you take me in your arms to tell me how proud of me you are and how much you love me. I love you Daddy, and I want you to know that you don't have to worry about protecting me anymore because of all the hurts you were also faced with, because my Heavenly Father has taken over and is refusing to let me go. I will never stop loving you, and my heart hurts every day because you are not there. But I'm going on to fulfill the life that my Heavenly Father has for me until I see you again.

Love your daughter, Michele; Daddy's little Girl

FOREWORD

Praise the Lord, for Michele sharing her life with you, and I pray that this book will be a blessing for you and yours. It is about her life as a child placed into foster care, and being subjected to abuse. You will read only part of what Michele will share with you, but I believe you will get the picture. Can you imagine, being in foster care and experiencing abuse there and then being rescued by your father. Also thinking that your life will be so much better because he is your biological father. Only to realize that after you have been brought home to him and his other family, that you continue to be even further abused by his then girlfriend, who would later go on to become his wife.

What a tragedy it must be to know that you are then invited to mold your life with our Lord and Savior Jesus Christ. And then being subjected to not being allowed to serve Him because your stepmother will not allow you to and go through even more abuse and not having the loving care from her parents, who Michele was trying to have a loving relationship with; to be met with more abuse and rejection. Then at the age of seventeen Michele knew she had come to the end of her road and did not want to go through any more pain so she decided to go to her mother and tell her that she thinks she should leave. Her stepmother agreed to let her go. Michele wanted to go out on her own to patch up her life and having the need of that loving relationship with her parents that she could not seem to get she finds herself in a place that she does not *know* but she knows it is better than going back home. Think of that, an innocent 17-year old finding life away from home where people would think was better than any other place but love did not live there for Michele so she desperately had to find it for herself. The fact that our Savior said, *"He would never leave us nor forsake us,"* is a reality in Michele's book. Just think of it, abuse, neglect, very little love from her parents, in the space of 17 years and the appearance of a lovely child desiring the worth that comes from parents, who just don't know; but the LORD knew. So we sing with the Heavenly Choir, look what the Lord has done and is doing, through Michele.

This book was written to share with men, women, and children alike. The Lord knew the plan and course that He was going to take in Michele's life to help someone else come through the pain, heartache, and disappointment of continued failure after failure. Also, to let the world know that God is truly with you and will never leave you nor forsake you ever. He can direct your path wherever He wants you to go, no matter the price you have to pay.

Pastor Richard T. Stonewall, Sr.

ACKNOWLEDGMENTS

Prophetess Juanita Bynum Thank you for your words of prophecy you gave to me 3 years ago, telling me I would tell my story. God knows that day that I never knew that it would be like this. It is because of you that my deliverance came over 11 years ago, and God knows I would of never gotten out of the hard place that I was in if it had not been for you. You are so dear and special to me, and it is because of you that I wear the black to remind me that I am always dying to this flesh. People would always say, "Look at her thinking she is Juanita Bynum!" They do not know that I do not have to be like you, because I have my own story to tell but everyone needs a mentor. I admire you so much for speaking the truth and living it too. I will always make sure I do that too. *God bless you woman of God!!!*

Pastor Clarence "Ernie" Stevens and First Lady Anne Stevens You are both very special to me and loved me and my children from the time I walked through the doors of the church 2 years ago. You both also played a vital part in my book. I never told you pastor about the book I was writing but one day in Bible study, you said there was someone in the ministry who is supposed to write a book, and I was already writing. I heard God that day confirm His word for me to continue with this book because it was going to help many people. He said that I would touch the lives of men, women, and children who have went through the same things that I have went through and this is what has them bound by the enemy and they can't break free.

First Lady Anne Stevens you were always so willing to listen to me, and I love your warm loving spirit. You both have loved me through some hard times and even now, I sit there and am still healing from deep hidden hurts.

Pastor, the day you took the towel off of my head and took the Neuse from around my neck in the spirit, an eagle flew that day. I have been soaring ever since, and I will never forget the home I have in case I want to fly back. Every time I present myself, I will have a scarf around my neck to remind me of the Neuse you took off of me. *God bless you!!!*

Thank you both for loving God enough to stand no matter what. You two are the best choice of leadership this side of Heaven. There is no one like you two. May God bless you both and your family abundantly above all you can think or ask. I want you to know that it is because of the both of you that I have learned what true parents are like.

Pastor Carlton "Mark" Avery, Sr. My "Spiritual Father" who birthed me out over 11 years ago. I could not have done any of this without you. The most precious years of my life, you made possible. My marriage was failing and I was truly going through some tough times. You have an awesome Healing and Deliverance Ministry, one that is not like most ministries. That was the place where I literally stole myself away like "The Woman with the Issue-of-Blood" and did not care what anyone thought or said. I know that is one place I can always come home to. You are a special father to me and I want you to know that. *May God Complete Your Work!!!*

Pastor Kim Davis You are someone very special to me that I will never forget. With you, I learned how to dress to impress and present myself in ministry. I will never forget the way you would always say, "Watch and do what I do." I was truly watching and learning how to be a lady too. It is because of you that I speak the way that I do. Thank you for being my "Spiritual Mother." You are truly a DIVA!!!

Bishop Gregory M. Davis Sr. There are no words to describe you. You were the tool that set the stage for me to be trained and groomed in the spirit. It was not easy for me to take flight. I remember the time that I was trying to be just like you, as most daughters are trying to be like their fathers, and I took flight and almost lost my life. God is truly good though and He had me to understand that I was not ready for that type of altitude that day, but now I am! I learned how to pose myself and move in the spirit with accuracy. Thank you father for teaching me how to fly. *God bless you real good!!*

Minister Kevron Tynes I want to thank you Minister Kevron for seeing something in me and pulling it out. I feel your spirit of such genuineness and your ability not to put up with any type of foolishness. That is what I love so much about you; don't ever change because God's not through with you yet! *God bless you!*

My "Spiritual Grandmother" Anna Anderson, I spend time with you on the phone talking every day. You have spent over 11 years with me on the phone praying. You never gave up on me or turned your back on me even when I knew I had to be getting on your nerves. If it had not been for you, I would not have written this book. Prayer is where it all had to start. You are an incredible person and incredible woman of God. I love you and I hope one day I can learn to be the woman you are. God bless you and may God give you long life and good health for many years to come. I always felt like we had a Mary and Elizabeth relationship because every time we talk it just seems like the baby just leaps in your womb. *May God bless you and keep you for many more years to come!!!!*

DEDICATIONS

Minister Donnie Miller - The one person who I credit this book to. You inspired me to write this book. I had heard many times before from people that I had a story to tell. But on one particular day while having a conversation with you, I heard something that I never heard before and that was: *"Michele, God wants you to write a book because you have so much in you, and you can help so many people just like you from getting into what you have already gone through or you can help them get out.* That is the day I decided to write the book. Thank you cousin, I love you so much.

May God bless you abundantly for your words!

TABLE OF CONTENTS

INTRODUCTION	i
CHAPTER 1 Life in Foster Care	01
CHAPTER 2 The Candy Man...My Uncle	04
CHAPTER 3 Reunited with My Daddy	06
CHAPTER 4 The Move...Our New House	08
CHAPTER 5 My Daddy Gets Married	15
CHAPTER 6 Bruce Lucado	17
CHAPTER 7 Love for God and My Earthly Father	19
CHAPTER 8 Turning My Room Upside Down	23
CHAPTER 9 I Adored My Daddy	27
CHAPTER 10 More About Bruce	30
CHAPTER 11 Not Allowed to Do Anything	33
CHAPTER 12 Playing with Myself	35
CHAPTER 13 My Biological Mother	38
CHAPTER 14 Finally Taken to the Doctors	42
CHAPTER 15 Getting Punished, My Father vs. My Mother	46
CHAPTER 16 My Junior Year	48
CHAPTER 17 Finally Allowed to Go Out with Thomas	51
CHAPTER 18 Started Running Away from Home	54
CHAPTER 19 My Life had Changed...I was Miserable	56
CHAPTER 20 My Stepmother was Not a Talker	60
CHAPTER 21 My Grandmother...My Stepmother's Mother	62
CHAPTER 22 My Older Brother Gets Abused	64

TABLE OF CONTENTS

CHAPTER 23 Daddies are Special to their Daughters 68
CHAPTER 24 Pastor Lucado and His Family 71
CHAPTER 25 Living Day to Day with a Monster...My Stepmother 73
CHAPTER 26 Feeling as if No One Loves or Cares...About Me 77
CHAPTER 27 My Diary 81
CHAPTER 28 The Final Chapter 86
ABOUT THE AUTHOR 90

INTRODUCTION

This book is about the early life of Michele E. Sweeney, and the years she lived as a young girl trying to make it in a dark world of a lot of pain and heartache. In the mist of it all, she was still trying to be the good girl that she desired to be.

From her birth to the age of 17 years of age, she had already experienced a lot of disappointments and hurts, which she had no control of. All she did was come here. Because Michele did not ask to be born here she'd sometimes ask the questions, "Why was I even born to be treated like this? Why do I have to be involved with a family like this? And how do I become the woman that I need to be when it looks like all of my family sees me as is the black sheep?"

There are no real answers to these questions, all she knows is that she was born for such a time as this, and she is going to try and make it the best way she can because she is strong, and very courageous. In addition, she is beautiful; at least that is what she keeps hearing everyone say to her.

Michele knows that she is a fighter and knows how to open up her mouth to get whatever it is she wants to say across to people. She can make it and she is determined to do so.

She has her older brother who she takes care of very well. So what if he doesn't talk that well, she understands him and no one will ever mess with him as long as she is his sister. The two of them together are all that they have and Michele will be the one to make everything all right. So what if their parents don't want them, they got each other and that is all that matters!

CHAPTER 1

Life in Foster Care

My childhood at age four, in foster care was very normal to me, I thought; until I had to leave and go home to my biological father and his girlfriend. I had an older brother whose name was, Paul, but I called him *Tubber*. He was named Paul after my daddy and grandfather. My brother was in the foster home with me. We were both very young when we went to the home. I cannot really remember just how old I was, but I do know that my father and mother's marriage split up and there was no place for us to go. We had to go somewhere, so foster care is where we ended up.

This took place back in the 60's when daddies were not allowed to have their children to raise by themselves because the law thought they could not adequately provide for them. My mother was sick at the time, and she could not properly care for us, although my daddy was trying very hard to get us, he had nowhere for us to go. My daddy's parents were both alcoholics, and he did not want them to raise us. Therefore, it was no choice left but for us to go into foster care.

My mother made the arrangements for us to be dropped off at the adoption agency in West Chester on a day that my daddy did not even know about. Before my daddy could arrive at the adoption agency, my brother and I had gone. My daddy was devastated, and he cried every day. Like I said I was too young to understand what had happened, but my brother was not. He was so affected by what had taken place that he could not talk well and had to have speech therapy to learn how to talk. As I got older in the foster home I was always strong and very talkative, so I thought everything was normal in my life. I thought the people I was living with were my real parents.

We were in the foster home, and our daddy did not even have knowledge of where we were. This must have been very hard for him. Back in them days the adoption agency would not even tell the father and mother where they were placing the child or children. My daddy worked very hard from the time we were both born, and he continued to work hard until he got us both back. He did not know if he would ever have success in getting us back, but he never gave up. I know that everyone has a purpose in life and to each person, there is a destiny. This was a part of my destiny I guess. I was not really feeling the hurt at this age though. I never remember missing my daddy or my mother. I know that was because I did not know them because I was too young. I do remember my brother and I getting abused by our foster mother. I remember times so vividly when I would get sick, she would put me in the basement in the dark and then sit my food and water on the step and make me come up to get the food after she opened the door placed and food and water on the step and then closed the door and walked away. She would make me get away from the door so that she could put the food down first. She did this because she told us she did not want to get sick with whatever made me sick. I remember one time when I had the chickenpox she did this. I also remember how my brother would come to the basement window to talk and play with me and keep me company. I felt like it was a game, but I knew it wasn't when my brother got the Chickenpox from me. After I got better I got to come out of the basement. However, my brother had to go in the basement and he cried all the time. This upset me more than anything. I could not understand why when I was in the basement that I did not see the bad in it. As I said earlier, I looked at it as being a game but when he went in there, he would cry all the time and did not want me to leave him. This part really did hurt me.

I would get in trouble for opening up the basement door, and for giving him food and for playing and talking to him. I could not wait until we could play together again. I remember tying his shoes for him and dressing him like I was his mother or something. He'd let me do everything for him. He hardly ever talked but I understood what he needed and I knew just what he wanted. We were connected like that. My brother was so traumatized from being here and not having our daddy and mother because he remembered them. He knew them and was ripped away from them in such a way that he never got the chance to say goodbye to our daddy and our mother. Our mother just gave us to people at the adoption agency and she did not even take the time to research anything concerning the whole process of adoption. She was just too sick to understand what she was doing, and she thought she was doing the right thing.

CHAPTER 2

The Candy Man...My Uncle

I was a very friendly girl, and I would talk to everyone I met. I do not remember too much about this place, but I do remember going to a certain mans house to get candy every day. I was the one who would knock on the door because my brother was too afraid. I did not know him but all I knew was that he would always give us both candy. He was always nice to me and my brother and I would talk to him at his front door and he would always give me candy. He would never let us in his house though. I did not know the whole time I was there that God had a plan. A plan was already set in motion even before I could understand what it was. My brother and I were going to his house so much that the man had a chance to build a rapport with us. He had a sister who lived in Downingtown, PA.; she was my daddy's mother. He called her up one day and they were talking. His sister was telling him how they could not find their grandchildren and how everyone was so upset. She went on to explain how his nephew and wife split up. It never occurred to the man to even stop to think that the children his sister was talking about were me and my brother. The man and his sister kept talking; and he became very curious about the situation.

I would go to his house everyday for candy, so he was able to get a good look at my brother and I. The man got on the phone said I think you need to tell Paul to come up here to see if these are his children because by the description of the them, I think they might be his. My grandmother got the address and told my daddy about what she heard, and they came to see if they we were indeed his children. Behold we were. (LOL)

The man that I had been going to visit every day was my uncle, my grandmother's brother and the woman was my Father's mother, my grandmother. Her name was Mary Stewart. See how God orchestrated all of this to happen? I believe this is the reason why I was not even worried and crying. God, had already covered me for the journey he was about to take me on. After the visit from my daddy, he was able to acknowledge that my brother and I were truly his children. He knew after that he had work to do. From that day, our daddy worked hard to make sure we would go home with him soon.

CHAPTER 3

Reunited with My Daddy

I do not remember visiting my daddy or my mother either, but I do remember going home with him because when we both arrived there he had new bikes for me and my brother to ride. We even had a younger brother; his name was Bob. My daddy and Bob's mother were not married, but they were living like common- law husband and wife. I remember there were so many children on the street where we lived. It was a small house that sat at the end of the street. It only had one bedroom but my daddy made it work for all of us to live in.

My daddy was such a loving and proud father. He took very good care of his family. He was a daddy that would do anything for his children. He worked hard to give us a good life. We never went hungry and we always had nice clothes on our backs. My father was fair, he told my brother and I that we did not have to call Bob's mother "Mommy" *(the woman that he lived with)* if we did not want to but we both did.

My half brother Bob was so tiny, and he accepted us both as his brother and sister right away. We all would play together and play with the other kids for hours before bedtime. I was happy and so was my older brother. I do not know what happened to our biological mother but all I did know is that now we have a family with our real father, and we had a stepmother who is our "new mother" that took the place of our biological mother. There were many fun days where we lived until I was about seven, and we moved out of this house into another house in the country. It was located in Downingtown still but now we were going to be living in a country area where there was a farm, horses and chickens.

CHAPTER 4

The Move...Our New House

My daddy worked until he could raise enough money for us to leave this one-bedroom house and move to a larger house. The area we moved to was called, West Bradford. It was a single-family home that had two bedrooms. I had my own bedroom now, and my brothers had their own bedroom. My parents slept on a pull-out couch in the living room. Our house and the house across the street were the only homes in the area at the entrance of that dirt road. There was a farm across the street with cows, horses, and chickens too. There was a big field to run and play in. There was a creek to put your feet in. A house about a quarter of a mile up the road was also near us but the people that lived there did not associate much with us. There was nothing wrong but they were just quiet people.

I always went to the woman's house that lived across the street from us; she would always let me in. Her name was Mrs. Lew; I remember the homemade yellow cakes that she would make that had the homemade white icing on them that would just melt in your mouth. The icing was real good; it was white and crunchy to the taste. She would always make them for my brothers and I. I would always go to her house everyday and just talk to her, and she would always make sure that I had a piece of her homemade cake. The cakes were made of fresh black walnuts that she would pick off of the trees out front of our house. Yummy!

I loved horses, and I would take my two brothers up the street to the farm. We would ride the horses and clean the stalls. We had a lot of fun doing this. My younger brother and I were the ones who would ride the horses for hours and hours, and then we would go home. The people who lived on the farm up the street had three children who were the same ages as us. We all got along very well. My life was full of a lot of happy times up until this point. I had what every child had I thought until one day all of that changed. I was about seven years old, and I remember my parents arguing a lot because my daddy would not come home at night. He was the type of man to stay out, but he always took very good care of us. I would always be up when he came in at night. And when he came home all they would do is argue and fight sometimes. I would lay there in my bed and just listen, but I did not understand why he stayed out.

  I remember my father drinking a lot; mainly, beer but it never interfered with him going to work and providing for his family. My stepmother and my daddy would argue, and then they would make up. They never stayed mad at each other long because the arguing would turn into other noises being made. I would hear them make up with each other. Once I knew that everything was all right then I would fall fast asleep. I never knew what they were doing but I knew everything was all right.

  Christmas was especially fun in our house because my stepmother was someone who knew how to make a holiday fun. She decorated our house for every holiday and made nice dinners too. I remember one time when we made cookies for Christmas, and she told us we had to go to bed early so that Santa Claus could come. I believed her too. In fact, I remember telling her that I heard Santa and his reindeer outside on Christmas Eve. We had a chimney too so when we got up the next day for Christmas and saw our presents you could not tell me that Santa Claus did not bring them down the chimney. My parents had a way of creating a real fantasy for me and my brothers. However, I do remember one Christmas when things for me did not seem so special and fun. When I got up on that day to open up my presents I did not have any; all that I had was coal in a stocking. I was so hurt by this and could not understand what I could have done that was so bad to make my parents give me this for Christmas. My brothers were both playing with their toys, and I was sitting there numb and hurting.

I felt I had a good life as far as I knew it to be up until this point because my birthdays were special and holidays were always made to be very special too. My stepmother made dinners that were filled with all the trimmings, and our house was always spotless. Everything was always in its place in our home. My mother used to always say her mother told her, "If it's a rag, let it be clean." I never forgot what she said that day.

My daddy and stepmother's relationship seemed like everything was okay except for the arguing and fighting at night. I could not understand how they would fight at night and argue when my daddy stayed out late hours almost every weekend, but they would always make up and everything would be okay again. This is when my life took a drastic turn for the worst. I remember one night my father stayed out and when he came home, I was still up waiting for him as I always did in my bed. I heard his car pull up in the driveway. My stepmother was also awake. When he came in the house, he started slamming the cabinet doors to the cupboards in the kitchen. My stepmother got up and told him to stop. I remember her saying, "Why do you always have to come in this house and start slamming cabinets? "No one has done anything to you!" My father made no reply to her; he just kept on slamming the cabinets.

After about an hour of him making the noise, he came into the living room where he slept at and went to sit down and said he had a headache. He said he wanted something for his headache. I had gotten up out of my bed by this time, and I was sitting on my father's lap. And I remember jumping up and saying to my stepmother, "I will get it." She quickly replied, "No, I will get it!" I said, "But I want to give it to him, please?" My stepmother gave it to me to give to him, and I gave the pills to my dad. Then he talked to me for a while, and then I was told to go to bed by my stepmother. She was in the dark in the kitchen when she said this. I remember getting up and walking towards the kitchen to go to my room and knowing that something was wrong with my stepmother. I remember it being so dark that I could barely see anything and that is when the horror began. Just as I reached for the handle, where the sliding door was that led to my room; my stepmother was standing on the other side of the doorway. She began beating me, scratching me on my face, punching me in the back, and saying to me, "Why did you do have to ask could you give those pills to your father and that she wanted to do it." I was so scared. Her nails were digging into my neck and back, and it felt like I was being attacked by a wild animal.

She continued to attack me for what seemed like hours, but I do not really know how long it lasted. She was pulling my hair and knocking me to the floor and pulling me back up and just hitting me and scratching me all over my face and neck. I could not understand what was going on because I was crying and asking her to stop and my daddy never came to help me. I have never been this afraid in my life and I was never the same after that night. It was as if a piece of my spirit was ripped right out of me.

My father never came to my rescue, and I know he heard me screaming and crying. He was my daddy, why didn't he make her stop? I wanted so badly for him to save me and he never did. He laid there in his bed and turned a death ear to what he knew had happened. She wasn't even my real mother. She was his girlfriend. Where was my mother? I know she would not have my stepmother do this to me? My daddy did nothing about this. She threw me onto my bed, and it felt like she hated me so much. I laid there in my bed shaking and shaking with no one to comfort me or take the pain away. I had to go to the bathroom so bad, and I was so afraid to get up and go because I did not want to make her do this to me again so I laid there until I just could not hold it any longer. Then I got up and tried to sneak to the bathroom and she came in the bathroom where I was, and I begged her not to hit me anymore and then I started to cry again. She grabbed me in her arms and said, "Why did you make me do that to you?" "Why did you make me hurt you like that?" I was so confused, and I hurt so badly that I could not even explain what she was talking about. What did I do? All I did was take my father pills for his headache that she gave me to give to him and that was all. What was so wrong with that? Did I deserve to be beat for loving my Daddy and wanting to help him when he was sick? I had always been a good girl and I always behaved well in school. I was a child who had straight A's in school and did it with ease. I was always trying to be good and listened to my parents whenever they told me something. I always did what my stepmother told me to do. How could she do this to me? He was my Daddy, my real father. I loved him with all my heart. I was Daddy's little girl. He was my hero.

I felt so empty now. While she was hugging me, I did not have any feelings. I felt numb and very confused. I could not even understand how I was supposed to be feeling because she had just beat and attacked me like some wild animal and then threw me on my bed like she literally could not stand me, and now she is standing here hugging me and expecting me to show affection back. All I felt for her as a stepmother was gone on this night. I could not even understand it. I never felt the same way towards her again after that night. She let me go and then she told me to go and say goodnight to my father who was still awoke when I said goodnight to him. I remember sitting down on the edge of the pullout couch where he was laying with my back turned to him and he continued to rub my back until he fell asleep. I never said a word to him, but I knew he knew what she did to me because if he didn't why did he rub my neck and back? He let her do this to me and did not even try to make her stop. What kind of daddy would do this to his daughter? I hurt so badly, and I was so afraid. I did not know what to do when he fell asleep. I knew I was going to have to get up from there and go to bed. I knew she was still up and I thought she was going to do it all over again. What was I going to do? She finally told me to go to bed and when I was walking back to my room she grabbed me and put her arms around me. And then started crying and saying to me, "Why did you make me do that to you?" Why doesn't she just leave me alone and let it go? I did not even know what to say so I just stood there and did not say a word. I was too afraid to make her angry again. After that day, I was never the same again. I never got close to my daddy again; I was too afraid.

Daddy, Where are you!

    My father and stepmother continued to go through their differences because he would continue to stay out late and come home which would make her fight and argue with him, but somehow they would always make up and things would be okay again. I never got up out of my bed again to even say goodnight to my father I would just lay there numb and did not care about what was going on with them. My brothers and I were really close especially me and my little brother; we did everything together. I never could understand why they never heard the fighting and arguing and why they never even heard her beat me like she did. I was too afraid to tell them because I did not want them to ever go back and tell her what I said. I was not about to have that happen to me again ever. The woman who lived across the street used to hear them fighting and she called the police sometimes because they would be fighting and arguing so much. She was really afraid because she did not know what was going on over our house. All I wanted to do at this point was just keep my stepmother as happy as possible so I did everything to stay out of her way. I would do everything she told me and just play outside with my brothers until it was time to come in. I hated it when it was time to come in because I did not even want to be around her after she hurt me. I hated it when my father went to work because it seemed like she would always pick at me and do things to hurt me.

CHAPTER 5

My Daddy Gets Married

I was still about 7 years old, and my daddy agreed to marry my stepmother. He could not get married to her before this because he was still legally married to my biological mother.

After the divorce was final, and my stepmother began to pressure my daddy into marrying her. I think somewhere deep down inside he did love her, but I do not believe he was ready for marriage again. When he was married to my biological mother, they had a bad marriage, so he did not want to rush into another marriage again. Besides, it wasn't like my father and girlfriend had a great relationship. He stayed out late at night a lot, and when he would come home, he would be drunk. Therefore, they would always argue and fight. Why would someone marry for reasons like this?

Then one day, it seemed like he just stopped. I do not know what happened but he stopped staying out late and decided to never go out again unless they were together. When they got married, my little brother was in the wedding but my oldest brother and I were not. They got married at a little church in Downingtown, called; Ebenezer Baptist Church. It was a nice wedding and both sides of the family were there. They also had a really nice reception. My daddy danced and they all had a nice time. Things were pretty good at our house, I guess. I did not talk to my stepmother too much, but I did help her with dishes, housework, and laundry because I had to. We stayed at this house for about a year after they were married and then we moved to a nicer house just a few miles up the road and around the corner from this one. It was a really nice house. It was a ranch house that sat on an acre and a half of land. I had my own room with a real door this time and my brothers shared a room. There were more kids to play with and we really had fun at this house. I was not sorry that we had moved here. My cousins lived right next door to us. They were related to me and my older brother on my biological mother's side.

CHAPTER 6

Bruce Lucado

I can't remember how old I was when we moved here, but I was still going to the same school. I was so happy because I was still able to see all of my friends.

I was starting to mature now and I was quite fond of a cute boy by the name of Bruce Lucado. I met him in West Chester at a parade on Market Street. I was playing near the courthouse with my stepmother and he ran over and asked me my name. I thought he was so cute. We continued to play together while we were at the parade and when it was over, I never thought I would see him again but by the start of the new school year started he was going to my school. Bruce and I called ourselves going together from that day on; as some would call it boyfriend and girlfriend. We would always play together. We were both in the same grade as each other. We were both in second grade. I remember playing outside on the playground and running after each other. He would always chase me around and play with me with his other friends. I was not doing very well in school by this time. I did not care much about my work as I used to. My grades started to go down from straight "A's" to "F's." That year my stepmother made me stay back. All of my friends went to the next grade and I had to stay back. Bruce was now in third and I was still in second. I hated the fact that I had to repeat the grade but I had no other choice. I was always good in school but now I had a attitude that I did not even care about school now. I would fight the kids in my class and cause problems in school. Everyone in my class was afraid of me. I was the fastest one in my class now out of the boys and girls and every time field day would come, I would win medals and ribbons. That is one thing I did like about staying back. I made the most of my years at this school after the day when Bruce left the school and went to middle school. He was in Junior high and I was still in elementary school. I felt like my whole world crumbled, all of my friends and boyfriend were gone. I could not wait until I could go to the Junior high school to be with them. The following year I was able to go.

I was in junior in high school having the time of my life. I was around other kids that I used to see and visit when I would go see my grandmother, who lived in Johnsontown. Bruce was in eighth grade now. There were a lot of new people in this school but he and I managed to still stay together. We were both on the track team, and we ran with each other when we could. There were a lot of pretty girls and nice-looking guys too, so we both drifted apart somewhat. No matter how long we were not together we always got back together.

I was starting to fill out a little. My hair was jet black and way down the middle of my back. The boys liked me a lot, but I was not interested in them.

CHAPTER 7

Love for God and My Earthly Father

I liked Bruce so much that I never really was interested in any other boy. I did not even know his father was a Pastor and that they had their own church? One day he asked me to go to church with them. I could not wait to ask my father and mother. I really wanted to go because I wanted to be with him. I went to church before, so I knew what church was all about. I would sing in the choir and go to Sunday school. I always liked church. My stepmother would send us to the church that her and my father got married in. She would sometimes go with us but most of the time she would take us and drop us off. My daddy would never go.

I was about 12 years old when I got saved through Bruce's parents. His father had his own church in West Chester, called Highway Gospel it was an Apostolic-Pentecostal church and this is where I really got introduced to who God was. I liked Bruce and when he would ask me to come to church, I would go but there was something different about this church and the experience I was having serving God. I felt a deep love for Christ and I wanted to go to church for more than seeing Bruce. I remember the old mothers in the church would make us sit on the first row and separate us from the boys. We could not even be allowed to get up to go to the bathroom unless it was an emergency because they would tell us that it was disrespectful to God and the word if we did this. There was a lot of discipline but I loved it. It did not seem like they were being mean to us but more as if they were training us for something. I had to wear skirts all the time and I was not allowed to go to church in pants; but at my other church I could.

During church service, they would shout, dance around, and speak in a funny language called "tongues." We would stay in church all night until the wee hours of the morning. I would leave for church at 7 pm, and I would not get home until sometimes around 4 am in the morning. I am not complaining because I loved it.

My stepmother would get angry if she saw me in a dress or skirt. Therefore, I had to sneak and wear them, but she would always catch me because when she did the laundry and all she would find is my skirts.

I was happier than I had ever been in my life and I did not even know why. However, one thing I was sure of was that I loved this church and the way they served God. I would go to church during the week and always on Sunday, until one day my stepmother told me I could not go anymore. I was so devastated, I thought my whole world was going to crumble; but I had to stop going. I cried and cried, but she still would not let me go. She said I could never go back and that was final. My father and her told me I could not serve God anymore. I could not understand any parents not letting their child go to church. I loved God with all of my heart and I could not understand why I did but I did. He was the only one who made any sense to me and made me really feel loved. I had a sense of peace that I could not explain and I was doing very well in school again. I was more loving and kind to everyone I came in contact with.

Bruce would visit my cousin's house, my cousins on my biological mother's side and his cousins on his father's side). He would come over their house quite often on the weekends and in the Summer. I really liked him a lot and I know God used him in the plan that He had for my destiny because he remained a very vital piece of the plan for many years after that. I could not understand meeting him one day at a parade and then him going to the same school as me and continuing to be at the same schools as me until he graduated and then went off to college.

I thank God for the Lucado's and how they were able to get me started on my way to where God was taking me. God will use whomever He sees fit to lead us to Him. They were definitely my "foundation" in every sense of the word. *The bible says in 2 Samuel 22:2, "The LORD is my rock and my fortress and my deliverer."* Therefore, He is our ROCK, FORTRESS and OUR DELIVERER. They were also that very thing to me in the natural.

I remember going to services with them in Philadelphia, and Pittsburg to the PAW Counsel. I had the most fun that I had ever had; I was spending time with them and going to church. I remember loving God so much and just accepting Him so easily as a young girl. I never struggled with the decision, whether I wanted to serve Him or not. I had a lot of hard times in my life and God was making those hard times feel better. The love I had for God at that age was close to the same type of love I had for my earthly father.

I adored my earthly father, and it was very easy for me to love him, even after I felt as though he did not protect me the way he should have when my stepmother beat me for just giving him aspirin for his headache. I had nothing to do with their problems and what was going on in their life. I only knew I loved my daddy, and I did not want him to hurt the night he asked me to get him something for his headache. All I wanted to do was help him, and look what it cost me? It cost me a relationship with my daddy forever.

CHAPTER 8

Turning My Room Upside Down

I had a room in a three-bedroom ranch house that was very nice. It was white with black shutters. My room was bigger and it had a door this time. The house that I moved from was smaller and the door was only a curtain that pulled. I would spend a great deal of time in this room because of always being on punishment. My room was baby pink like my room in my other house. I had a very small closet with only a few clothes and shoes to wear. My bed was a full size bed with a lot of room for me and my stuffed animals. I had a pink furry rug on the floor that I loved to sit on because it felt good on my feet. There was a window by my bed that I would always sit and look out of when I was sitting on my bed. I would sit there for hours and hours just coloring and reading my books. I would only be allowed out of my room for dinner and to do chores. I always made sure that I took all of the time that I could to stay out of my room because I was so tired of sitting in there. There was no one to play with or talk to.

On Saturdays in my house, my stepmother would clean our house. I would always have to help her clean the house. Everything was on one floor so it was very easy to clean it was just that I did not want to do it all the time and be in there with her. I was so hurt by everything and feeling as if nothing I did was right that I did not know what to do half of the time or even what to say. I do not remember praying much while I was in my room because I felt like God had given up on me. He never made sure that

I was okay nor did He ever try to get me out of this horrible situation. The times that I would be in my room I would be so tired of being in there that I would sometimes just leave things a mess. When I would clean the room, everything would be in place and in order. I would play in there with my dolls and books and sometimes I would go through the draws and even look for things and the clothes would get messed up. I would not fix it back so things would then be out of order. My stepmother would go in the room when I was not there and when I would come back and go in my room I would find everything on the floor and she would come to the door and say, "Now clean it all up and but it all back where it belongs!" I would be so upset. The first time she did this to me, I cried so bad because I could feel the hatred and rage in her and it scared me so bad. I was terrified of her. I had such a hard time dealing with the fact that someone could be so cruel and mean to people. I did not deserve this kind of treatment. I was a good girl. Daddy, where are you? Where are you when I need you to be there for me to hold me and comfort me when I am in so much pain? The room was literally a disaster area and everything was on the floor. You could not even see the floor because of all the mess. All of my clothes that were in the closet were on the floor, along with everything else that was in the closet. Every dresser draw was thrown on the floor with everything that was in it. The bedding on the bed was on the floor too. Nothing was left where it belonged but the mattress. All of the things that I had on the top of the dresser that were mixed in with the pile of mess on the floor. I could not think to even try to figure out where everything went. I knew my stepmother was mad and I had to pick all of the stuff up and place it back where it went or she was going to come in my room and do something to me. I did not even want to think of what that might be. I began picking up the mess. It took me hours to finally get all of the stuff picked up off the floor. No one could imagine what I felt like now. I was picking things up off the floor and I noticed a necklace that a friend of mine had given me and it had all of this black stuff on it that was getting all over my hands and the necklace was even broken into several pieces. I cried so hard because it was special to me. Now what was I going to say to my friend when he asked me about the necklace? How could I tell him that my stepmother broke the necklace and put some kind of black stuff all over the necklace? All of the stuff that was happening to me just kept getting more and more crazy to me that sometimes I thought I was going crazy. I thought it was my imagination playing tricks on me. I fought long and hard to keep myself together mentally so I did not lose my mind. I was still nice to her and treated her nice because I was not a mean person anyway and I did not want to make her more upset with me. I just needed so much love now and someone to hold me to ease the pain. She painted such a horrible picture about me in the minds of my two brothers that they would not even come near me to even talk to me. My stepmother continued to turn my room upside down from that day on until I looked forward to her doing it. I knew every time I came into my room what to expect. I already planned on picking the stuff up off of the floor. It just seemed so normal. What was my stepmother trying to do to me? She was always trying to make me be like her but I did not want to be this way. Everyone in the house listened to everything she told them to do even if it was wrong they would do it. My daddy listened to her to the point where he did not even care about what she was doing to me. I was his child, his own flesh and blood; and it was as if he never considered the things she was doing to me.

CHAPTER 9

I Adored My Daddy

I would always go over my cousin's house to play with them and I would go over their house whenever I knew that Bruce was over there. We were always able to talk and laugh with each other. They had an in-ground swimming pool built so we would all go swimming. We did other things like ride our bikes together, played football, and talk. I was a tomboy back in the day so everything the boys did, I did. And I must admit, no one could even tell that I was a girl. I played tackle football just like the boys did, and they tackled me too. However, I was getting older now, and I was starting to fill out. I was looking like a young lady now, so sometimes when I played too rough with the boys, I would run home and tell my dad that my chest hurt, and he would say, "Michele, you have to stop playing with those boys so rough." He would call my brothers into the house and tell them not to play so rough with me because I was a girl, and some things were changing on me.

I am now about 14 years old. Bruce came over to my cousins' house to visit. He and I were quite fond of each other and at this time I was not going to church anymore because my mother would still not allow me to. Therefore, I literally thought that God did not want anything to do with me. My stepmother made me believe that God was not good, and He was not the person I needed in my life. I actually believed it too, because when she beat me that day I did not remember God coming to protect me. I needed Him to protect me that day, but He did not. Where was God at that night when I was hurting badly, and I felt like I wanted to die? Daddy, where were you when I needed you that night too? I was very confused and mixed up that I did not even know what to think. I literally felt numb again.

Bruce and I were playing together and I can remember how cute he was. He was even starting to get muscles and stuff. I was also changing; at that time, I had long silky black hair that fell way down my back in curly locks. I was about 115 pounds and I was told all the time that I was the prettiest girl around. I sure did not see what everyone else saw. I sure did not seem pretty.

I used to always play with Bruce, but I never touched him in any way and he never tried to touch me. However, things changed and on this particular day when we were talking to Bruce he asked me if he could have a kiss. I was so scared and nervous, but I really liked him so I decided to kiss him too. I did not really know much about kissing because a kiss to me was just two people who kissed each other on the lips. I was doing everything I could do to stall because I was nervous, and a part of me wanted to do it, but a part of me did not. Then he finally made the first move; Bruce grabbed me and he started kissing me. The worst thing happened. He stuck his tongue in my mouth. I was like, "Oh my God!" I remember quickly stopping him and asking, "What are you doing?" He said, "I'm teaching you how to French kiss." He was the first person to teach me how to kiss. He was a very good kisser, and he would always tell me that no one could kiss the way I could. It was like forbidden fruit that day, I was hooked. It felt so nice and his breath was so clean and fresh. I just wanted to keep kissing him and kissing him. That was all we would do whenever we were together. He would never try to have sex with me though.

Bruce, at that time was older than I was by one year. He seemed so mature and outgoing and that is what attracted me to him. I remember him being my boyfriend off and on from second grade up until he graduated from high school. We never really got serious though because I was not allowed to see him. My parents did not like him. My daddy would always say, "There is something about that boy!" I did not care that my daddy did not approve; I liked him. I could not understand how my father would think there was something about him; being as though he did not even know how to protect me. Where was he, how could he say such a thing about someone else?

CHAPTER 10

More about Bruce

I would always go over my cousin's house to play with them and I would go over their house whenever I knew that Bruce was over there. We were always able to talk and laugh with each other. They had an in-ground swimming pool built so we would all go swimming. We did other things like ride our bikes together, played football, and talk. I was a tomboy back in the day so everything the boys did, I did. And I must admit, no one could even tell that I was a girl. I played tackle football just like the boys did, and they tackled me too. However, I was getting older now, and I was starting to fill out. I was looking like a young lady now, so sometimes when I played too rough with the boys, I would run home and tell my dad that my chest hurt, and he would say, "Michele, you have to stop playing with those boys so rough." He would call my brothers into the house and tell them not to play so rough with me because I was a girl, and some things were changing on me.

I am now about 14 years old. Bruce came over to my cousins' house to visit. He and I were quite fond of each other and at this time I was not going to church anymore because my mother would still not allow me to. Therefore, I literally thought that God did not want anything to do with me. My stepmother made me believe that God was not good, and He was not the person I needed in my life. I actually believed it too, because when she beat me that day I did not remember God coming to protect me. I needed Him to protect me that day, but He did not. Where was God at that night when I was hurting badly, and I felt like I wanted to die? Daddy, where were you when I needed you that night too? I was very confused and mixed up that I did not even know what to think. I literally felt numb again.

Bruce and I were playing together and I can remember how cute he was. He was even starting to get muscles and stuff. I was also changing; at that time, I had long silky black hair that fell way down my back in curly locks. I was about 115 pounds and I was told all the time that I was the prettiest girl around. I sure did not see what everyone else saw. I sure did not seem pretty.

I used to always play with Bruce, but I never touched him in any way and he never tried to touch me. However, things changed and on this particular day when we were talking to Bruce he asked me if he could have a kiss. I was so scared and nervous, but I really liked him so I decided to kiss him too. I did not really know much about kissing because a kiss to me was just two people who kissed each other on the lips. I was doing everything I could do to stall because I was nervous, and a part of me wanted to do it, but a part of me did not. Then he finally made the first move; Bruce grabbed me and he started kissing me. The worst thing happened. He stuck his tongue in my mouth. I was like, "Oh my God!" I remember quickly stopping him and asking, "What are you doing?" He said, "I'm teaching you how to French kiss." He was the first person to teach me how to kiss. He was a very good kisser, and he would always tell me that no one could kiss the way I could.. It was like forbidden fruit that day, I was hooked. It felt so nice and his breath was so clean and fresh. I just wanted to keep kissing him and kissing him. That was all we would do whenever we were together. He would never try to have sex with me though.

Bruce, at that time was older than I was by one year. He seemed so mature and outgoing and that is what attracted me to him. I remember him being my boyfriend off and on from second grade up until he graduated from high school. We never really got serious though because I was not allowed to see him. My parents did not like him. My daddy would always say, "There is something about that boy!" I did not care that my daddy did not approve; I liked him. I could not understand how my father would think there was something about him; being as though he did not even know how to protect me. Where was he, how could he say such a thing about someone else?

CHAPTER 11

Not Allowed to Do Anything

I was about 15 or 16 years old now, and I just remember not being allowed to do anything. My stepmother would not let me talk on the phone to my friends nor have friends over. I was so upset at the life that I had to deal with. All of the friends I had at school were allowed to date and talk on the phone and I was constantly teased for not being allowed to.

As you could guess, I wasn't allowed to date Bruce so I would sneak and call him when my stepmother went to work. I remember talking to him for hours on the phone. Back in them days if someone wanted to break through the line they could call the operator up and tell them that you had to break through the line because they had an emergency. Therefore, my stepmother would have the operator interrupt the line when Bruce and I were on it. I would get in so much trouble, but I did not care because it seemed like nothing I did pleased her anyway. She was so mean and hateful to me. She never treated my brothers this way just me. My older brother was never around. All he would do is go over his friends house who were all white and stay there until he had to come home. He agreed with everything my stepmother would say even if he had to go against me to do it. He got me in trouble plenty of times by telling her things that I did not even do just to please her and be able to do what he wanted. I would keep the peace by just staying out of her way and saying as less as possible. I would walk around the house and ignore her. At times, I would never even say anything to her for months, and she wouldn't say anything to me. I did not do this to be smart but I just did not know how to talk to her. How do you talk to someone who has treated you so bad and never made you feel loved or respected? I was a little girl and I needed her to treat me with love and respect, after all; she was the one who came into my life. I did not ask her to come into my life.

CHAPTER 12

Playing with Myself

I was going through a lot of changes and feeling a lot of feelings and at times I did not even know what I was feeling. I started to feel desires that I had never had before. Desires and urges to have sex. My stepmother never sat me down and had a real healthy conversation with me about sex and what I would feel when it was time for me to have sex with someone I really cared for or how my body would feel when I wanted to have sex so I did not know what was going on with me. I began to touch myself on my breasts and then on my vagina to satisfy the feelings that I had and make them do away. I would do this a lot and then I began to like it so much that I found that the more I did it the more I would want to do it. I was never allowed to date and my stepmother always made me feel like sex was bad and nasty. She would tell me that it was too. She said it was "dirty." Why did I have these feelings that felt so pure and warm but she would say it was not right to touch boys and that they were only after one thing from me and after they got it they would talk about me and leave me. I would listen to my daddy talking to my two brothers and giving them condoms to telling them to go and have sex. He would be laughing and joking around with them but telling me to sit there and keep my legs closed. He would say you are not allowed to have sex. I would begin to wonder to myself if the people my brothers were having sex with were girls. If I was being told to stay home and keep my legs closed than were other girls being told to do the same thing? They did not know what I needed love too. I should have been getting love from my daddy and stepmother that was the, right kind of love; that would have filled the void that I had to masturbate. I should not of been even doing this. Why was I doing this to myself was it because of what my daddy's sister did to me? I went through this most of my younger childhood at my grandparents house and not I was doing this to myself. Imagine something that felt so bad and wrong then was feeling so good and right now. My stepmother knew that I was masturbating and one day when I went into the bathroom she had a perfume bottle that I had been using to touch my vagina with that she drew on a piece of construction paper sitting on the back of the toilet seat and when I walked in to go to the bathroom I almost passed out. Something came over me that made me feel sick to my stomach. I stood there and could not imagine this picture staring back at me and me thinking to myself, "She knew my secret." This was my secret that no one was supposed to know about. I felt so raped and violated that day. How could a stepmother do this to a child she was raising? She would not let me date nor could I have any friends. What was I going to do? I had feelings that I could not even control. I needed love that I could not get from anyone. The picture even said, "The Art of Masturbation" on it. I was not feeling like myself right now, and how was I going to go out of the bathroom and face her now after this. I know she knows now. I finally did leave the bathroom and go back into my room. I just lied on my bed and did not even move. I heard my stepmother go into the bathroom after I left it, and then I waited, and then I went back into the bathroom to see if the picture was still there. It was gone. My father and brothers were all home and I did not want them to go in there and see this picture. The picture looked like an artist had drew it. I did not even know that my stepmother could draw like that. I was never the same that day and I did continue to masturbate because that was the only form of love that I could find. It helped me to sleep at night and take away the pain that I was feeling most of the time.

CHAPTER 13

My Biological Mother

My biological mother I never got to see much. However, what I remember most about seeing her was that she was light-skinned, very fat, and her hair was never combed. And she would always be coming out of her bedroom from being asleep. I guess I was kind of glad she did not get a chance to raise me because God only knows how I would have turned out? My brother and I would only see her when my daddy allowed us too.

I resented my biological mother for not taking care of my brother and I because she had no idea what she allowed to happen to us. I was living with a stepmother who looked the part, so everyone thought. We had a nice house and her and my daddy drove nice cars, but no one knew the real story. We only visited her once a year, if that. I remember one time she called our house and told my stepmother she had presents for us and my stepmother took us to get them. When me and my older brother were opening the presents my little brother started crying and saying, "Where are my presents?" My stepmother just looked at him and said, "Don't worry you have me and that is all you matters?" I got so upset with her comment that I threw the presents down and cried to her and said, "I do not want the presents!" She would always find a way to ruin every happy moment I had by saying or doing something to show she was upset. She would not allow me to have a normal relationship with my own daddy and now she was even angry when my own mother gave me and my brother gifts. I could not do anything right in this house. Every time I even tried to explain to my daddy how she would never talk to me when he was at work and how she would never treat me right, he would always say, "Michele stop trying to wreck my marriage." I was not trying to wreck anyone's marriage all I wanted was to be treated with love. This is something that I never felt from either of them like I should have. A nice house in a good neighborhood, clothes, and food on your table does not mean that you are loved. These are just things and things don't mean love. Love is caring for each other and talking to people in a kind voice; not always having someone say mean things to you in a harsh tone of voice. No one wants to be treated this way. This is the only language I knew. Everyone was always hollering around me or at me. I could never make my own choices either. I always had to do what my stepmother wanted me to do. I did not want to do everything that she wanted, I had my own needs and wants and some of the stuff she liked I did not like at all. Everything I decided on no matter what it was she did not like it.

I remember one time when I was about 16 years old; a friend of my older brother who was quite fond of me and wanted to take me to his senior prom. I was only in the 9th grade at the time when I met him and I thought he was the ugliest guy ever. He was not my type at all. My stepmother liked him and she wanted me to go with him. I had to go with him even if I did not want to. My older brother used to hang out with him and another guy named Thomas Raines. He wanted to date me too. I did like him though. He was short like my father, dark-skin, and he had such a pretty smile. I wanted to date him, but my mother would not let me. I can remember many times when guys would ride their bikes to my house, walk, and even get rides just so they could come and see me, and my stepmother would always run them away. She would tell them, "Don't you ever come back here again!" We lived so far out in the country and I was not even the one who was inviting them to come see me. It wasn't like she was saying I couldn't date she just wanted me to date the boys she liked. I thought at this point in my life that all step-parents must do is come into your life if your biological parent's marriage do not work out and just be there to cause pain and hurt to you for something that you have done wrong. All my life now has been so complicated and confusing and none of it is making any sense to me at all.

One time when I was at the high school for indoor track, I remember my stepmother came to the school and some boys from the Coatesville track team ran down to Downingtown school just so they could see me. The run was about seven miles away. I do not know where my stepmother came from but she jumped out of the car and began hollering, screaming, and beating me and making me get in the car to go home. I was so embarrassed because the football team saw it, and they began laughing at me. The next day, they all had made up a song me about what had happened. My brothers were on the team too and so was Bruce. I was so upset. I was 16 years old; I was not some girl who was out there having sex with a bunch of people; I was still a virgin. I remember the time when my so-called-friend called my house and told my stepmother I was pregnant by Tom Robson, who was a guy on the football team who liked me at the time, but I was not. I was still a virgin and did not even have an interest in having sex at this time. I would kiss a guy, but that was it. My stepmother was so convinced that I was pregnant because I had been sick on the stomach and could not eat. It hurt me to walk I was so sick I had to go to my daddy and tell him I was sick. He would work long hours because he was a truck driver, and when he would come home he would say to me, "You didn't go to the doctors yet?" I would just said, "No!" I swore at that age that my daddy was afraid of my stepmother because he would never say anything to her about how she treated me, and I know he knew. I know he did. This was my real daddy, how could he let a stranger, who was not my real mother treat me this way?

CHAPTER 14

Finally Taken to the Doctors

This went on for what seemed like so long. After about two weeks my father realized that something was wrong, my stepmother finally took me to the doctors. I had never been to this doctor before. I remember the doctor telling me to take off my clothes, and I had to urinate in a cup; I did not know what was going on. I was so scared that day. She even checked my private area and looked at it with a light. I did not know why she did this. I had to take off all my clothes and put on a gown.

After the doctor examined me, we went home and nothing else was ever said except that I had a urinary tract infection (UTI which is a bacterial infection that affects part of the urinary tract), and I had to take medicine for it. I could not even go to school this whole time because I was so sick, but I was glad when I finally could.

When I returned to school, everyone was looking at me funny and talking about me. I would not even talk to the girl who spread the rumor either. She was my cousin too. How could she do this to me? Things got pretty heated between everyone and they all decided to try to fight me after school one day. I wish you could have seen all of the girls after me. I was all by myself with all the black girls who went there; including my Aunt Sabrina, who was my biological mother's sister. I could not believe it and to this day, I do not deal with her. There were about thirty black girls trying to fight me that day.

Daddy, Where are you!

I ran and called my stepmother to come pick me up. She came and picked me up and never knew what happened to me because I never thought to even tell her. She treated me so bad herself so why would I tell her about this? No one ever knew my stepmother was treating me like this because my father would always make us respect and love her. I learned to hide the pain and hurt, and make her look like a great mother, but she was far from that. I purposely got bad grades on my report card just so I did not have to go to the prom with my brother's ugly friend. I wanted to go with Thomas Raines (the fine one), the one I liked; not him. My mother was very good friends with my brother's friend's mother, and one day they had a senior party at his house. My stepmother let us all go and I must admit I had a good time. I tried so hard to date him but I was just in so much pain inside that I just could not fake. I was not attracted to him at all. He was nice to me though.

I knew I was a nice girl. I also knew how to carry myself and talk to people. But why couldn't I fit in with what was going on? I did not feel nice or like a good girl. I had never been told that I was good. All I ever heard were bad things, and had bad things done to me. Many people thought the world of me, and they treated me with the utmost respect. However, I did not feel any of this. I felt ugly and horrible inside. I know I could have been a nicer girl at least it would have been more real if I would have been treated better as a younger child. I had the mind-set to be good and a nice girl but so much damage was done to me that whatever effect the damage did to me was literally coming out of me inside my head. I always felt ugly and like I did not even like myself. No matter how much people would tell me I was pretty and a good girl it did not feel like it to me. This only upset me more when it was being said to me. The only one who was ever really able to talk to me and have me feel good was my grandmother. She understood me, and she would always say, "If your father and mother treat you bad just come and tell me." I would tell her but she would just make me something special to eat and talk to me for hours. My whole world crumbled one day when I lost my grandmother to death. She had been sick for years with what the doctors thought was sugar diabetes. She kept on having these seizures that would make her head shake for about 10 minutes and she would just stare into space. Once the seizure were over she would just go back to where she left off. She would be weak though. The seizures started happening more and more often so my father and mother agreed to take her to have an MRI done on her. This is where they lay you in a long tube with nothing but a gown on and take computerized images of your whole body. I remember my grandmother leaving that day to go get the test and when she came back my parents told us she had to have surgery on her head because she had a brain tumor. She had to get the surgery right away because the tumor was located above her nasal area and the doctors said it would eventually come through her nose passages and out of her nose if they did not operate right away. I guess this explained why my grandmothers forehead always stuck out so far and it seemed like it was getting worse as the years went by. My grandmother left to go to the hospital a week later. My father, grandfather, his brother, and both of their wives took her to Chester County Hospital. My father said when she walked in she turned around and looked outside and said, "This is the last time I will be walking in here and walking out." He said she just turned around and walked in the door and never said another word. I was in 10th grade at the time my grandmother went in the hospital. She got the operation to have the tumor removed and they had to shave off all of her hair to do it. My stepmother had the one long braid and the hair that they shaved off of the top of her head in a plastic bag. We all got to see her after the surgery was over. I remember her just holding my hand and a tear just went down her face. She smiled at me and I knew everything was going to be all right, at least this is what I thought. The day after the surgery my brothers and I were in school and my daddy came to pick us up and told us we had to go see my grandmother in the hospital because she had a heart attack and was now in a coma. I got so upset and we all started to cry. When we arrived at the hospital everyone of my family members were there, from my cousins to all of my Aunts and Uncles from both sides of the family. They were all in the waiting room waiting to get in to see her. I remember when it was my time to go in and see her I read her Psalms 23 from the King James Bible. I said a prayer for her too. I remember asking Jesus to heal my grandmother and let her go home. My grandmother stayed in a coma for over two months and then one day a call came for the family to go to the hospital to pull the plug, which was a machine that supplied artificial life support because there was nothing else the doctors could do for her. My grandmother passed away in April 1980. I thought I was going to die that day. She was my best friend, the only one who ever really cared about me. The funeral was planned, and she took her final ride in a beautiful white Hurst with all of us following her. She had on a beautiful baby blue dress with a hat to match and beautiful baby blue slippers on her feet. I had no real feelings at this point and did not seem to care what happened from this point on.

CHAPTER 15

Getting Punished, My Father vs. My Stepmother

I can remember my father struggling with cigarette smoking and my brother and I hiding his cigarettes. I would always show him pictures of lung cancer patients and start crying while telling him that I did not want to lose him this way. I would run in the bathroom and flush them down the toilet. This went on for a while until my father became so mad that he demanded that my younger brother and I give them back. He threatened to beat us if we didn't, and I knew he was serious, so I did. He told us both not to do this again or we would be punished.

My father had a different way of punishing us, but you knew you were only getting punished because you did something you had no business doing. He would laugh before he did it. Then he would just grab you and beat you, and then make you go to your room. I did not care if he punished me as long as it was because of something that I deserved to be punished for. We never really got a beaten from our father, just mostly put on punishment.

When my stepmother punished me, it seemed like she hated me so much. I could feel the evilness behind every word. I remember one time when she was painting outside, and I came near her to kiss her she said to me, "You kiss me with the kiss of Judas. I know that he was one of Jesus' disciples, and he was the one who betrayed Jesus on the night of His capture before He was crucified. I could not understand her saying this to me. My uncle was outside cutting the grass that day, and she said it very loud and I was in fear that he had heard her. Therefore, I was hurt even more. How could she say this to me? Some of the things that she said to me seemed so crazy, and I thought to myself why do people have such mean hearts? My heart was not like this even after all I had been through. I always managed to keep a good heart. My stepmother would never take me anywhere with her unless my brothers or my daddy was there.

She started going out in the car with my little brother and leaving me home. My older brother was never there because she would always let him go with his friends whenever he wanted. He was never home. All I got to do was work. I was always on punishment too, for little things. I just wanted a normal life and to be happy. I remember being happy when I was going to church, and after that stopped it seemed like my whole life changed for the worse. You know it's funny because I looked up to my stepmother, and there were things that she did that I did that I did want to be like her, like the way she would keep her house and cook. She even dressed nice. But what she did not know is that I always watched her and the things that she would do. I knew I did not want to be like her because she was so mean. I did not want to be like this. I had a good heart, and if I could just get away from all of this, I could have a happy life and live the way I wanted to.

CHAPTER 16

My Junior Year

I was in the eleventh grade now, and I cannot even make sense of anything. I do not even want to go to school. I was getting bad grades, and I just did not have any interest in school. It was my junior year, and I do not even care about it. I do not want to do anything. At this point, I do not know what to do. My brothers get all the attention and love. They get to do everything, but I am like the black sheep of the family. My stepmother buys them everything. I can probably count on two hands how many outfits I have in my closet and most of them are from the previous years. I had to make do with everything. I knew how to make it work though. No one ever knew because my stepmother would always say to me, "You better not tell nobody what is going on in this house!" I was so afraid that I never did. Besides, who was I going to tell? The people I did tell in the family did not even believe me. They must have thought I was the crazy one for making up such crazy stuff. I must have been a good storyteller to make up these kinds of stories that's how crazy they were. I literally felt like Cinderella in the Walt Disney story. There was no excuse for any child to be treated like this.

My stepmother stayed dressed every day in new clothes, and she had a lot of shoes and pocketbooks to go with her clothes. She always dressed nice when she went out. My daddy did not have any clothes to wear. My mother dressed herself, but she did not try to be the type of woman to encourage her husband to dress. My daddy stayed in his work clothes and always worked around the house, if he wasn't asleep. He was a very affectionate man to my stepmother and displayed it openly to us when we were little. He would come from behind her and start hugging and kissing her. And then they would go off into the bedroom and close the door. They were very open with their love for each other. I was not jealous of that, but I did want love to be expressed to me from my daddy, and it very rarely was.

My stepmother would always come around whenever my father and I were together and give off a strong vibe as if she could not stand it. What was she trying to say to me, or was it being directed to the both of us? We would just get away from each other when she came around to avoid a potential problem. I really wish I could explain how I felt being a child in this house, in this life that no one seems to understand. Was I the only child out there going through this?

What plan did God have for my life? The bible says in Jeremiah 29:11 that *He knows the plans He has for us*. What plan did He have for me? My stepmother never really deposited anything positive inside me from the time I was beaten by her until this time in my life, and maybe I did not let her because I did not trust her because of all the bad things she did to me. I totally leaned and depended on my daddy for everything, even though he did not respond to me. Whenever I had a problem or a question to ask, I asked him. I did not care what it was. He would always say go ask your mother, but I would never do it, so I never got the answers I needed.

How I longed for a mother to teach me things, and let me wear her clothes and her jewelry and perfume I remember my stepmother getting mad with me because when she would do the laundry, she could smell her perfume on my clothes. I would always be punished for that, during the time when I was going to the Lucado's church. They only allowed us to wear dresses or skirts, and I had enough skirts to wear to school and church. I would only have dresses and skirts in the laundry when my stepmother washed clothes and my mother would find the skirts, and I would be punished for that. I just could not do anything right in her eyes, and I really did not possess any of the qualities that she had. She was not my real mother so how could she expect me to be like her? Even from a small child I knew something was so wrong with her and I did not desire to be like that. I would always wonder what God would do to me if I acted like that and what would He let happen to me. Don't get me wrong things were not always bad; we went on vacation to the beach every year for a week, and went to all different amusement parks in the Summer. We also went to the movies and out to dinner at nice restaurants, but I was just so unhappy after everything was all over. I was just there because everyone else was there.

CHAPTER 17

Finally Allowed to Go Out with Thomas

I can remember so clearly, when I was finally allowed to go out with a guy that I really liked. His name was Thomas Raines, and my daddy had him come to the house and ask his permission to take me out. So, he came and talked to my father, and my father told him you can take out my daughter, but you better have her back in this house by 8 o'clock pm and no later. This may sound funny, but that is exactly how I wanted to be treated, like a perfect lady. I wanted to do things right, and I wanted to remain a virgin until I was married. I wanted to marry the right man someday, have his children, and live happily ever after. This is what most young girls want.

My daddy asked him where he was taking me, and he told him to McDonald's. My father said okay; and then we left and went to McDonald's.

Thomas had me back by 8 o'clock and no later. He asked me when he walked me into the house if he could he kiss me and I said, "Yes." As we started kissing he would not let me go, and then he took my hand and made me feel his penis. I was so afraid that I ran into the house. I had never put my hand on that part of a person before, and I was scared to death now. I was still young and still a virgin.

When I came into the house from the laundry room area where he walked me to the door my daddy was asleep. He worked really long hours, and he was tired and slept most of the time. I just wanted to do everything right like my daddy wanted me to do so I did not disappoint him. He did not understand it was hard for me to try to please my stepmother, but my father was not that hard to deal with in certain areas. She on the other hand never gave me a chance. I do not know what kind of girl she thought I was, but I was not the little girl she made me out to be. I was a nice girl, that was trying so hard to stay nice in the mist of all the bad things that were going on with me. All of the stuff I was dealing with were other people's problems that they were letting come out on me.

I never told my daddy what Thomas had done to me because I still liked him, but I did not want to have sex with him or do things like making me touch and feel on his private parts. I just wanted him to get to know me and continue to take me out to have fun. But, Thomas was a senior, and he was not trying to talk; he was trying to have sex. I was some young pretty girl that he was going to try to get to first I guess that's what he thought? My daddy would have killed him if I had told him that, but I did not tell because I knew I was not going to do anything with him anyway.

The next day Thomas called me on the telephone. When we were on the phone, my stepmother was listening in on our conversation. We knew this because we both heard her hang up the phone after he and I were discussing the part about him making me touch his penis. I was so scared at this point, that I remember her coming out of her room and saying to me, "Here take these because you are going to need them!" I had never seen what she threw down on the table before, but when I read the pack, I did begin to understand what they were. She gave me condoms and birth control pills. I thought to myself, what kind of a girl does she think I am? If she heard the conversation right, she would have known that I did not make this happen, and I was telling the boy that I did not like what he did. He was saying that he was sorry, and he would never do it again. How could she as my stepmother try not to console me, but instead accuse me of wanting to have sex? I just remember feeling so violated by my stepmother and Thomas.

I felt so misunderstood. Why did everyone think that I was this tramp of a girl, and I wasn't? Why did it seem like everyone was trying to change me and make me what they wanted me to be? I was a good girl, and that is what I was trying so much to hang on to. Where was God? And why did He keep on letting all of these bad things happen to me? The things that I wanted to do, He wouldn't let me do, and the things that I did not want to do, He let happen. At least, this is how I saw it. None of it made any sense at all.

CHAPTER 18

Started Running Away from Home

Things were getting so bad that I started running away from home. I did this about three different times. I was just so tired of being treated the way that I was being treated. Therefore, I thought that if I ran away and went to stay somewhere else things would change for me.

My daddy always found me and brought me back home though. I remember one time running to a guy's house that I liked. He was what you call a bad-boy. He was older than I was by one year, and he was very mature and he knew the streets. He would ride his motorcycle down the road from my house, so he could meet me. His name was Kevin Baggs.

Kevin lived in Johnsontown of Downingtown. He was quite fond of me, and I liked him too because he seemed so cool. I would go for rides on the back of his motorcycle, and then he would take me back home and leave. But, one time my older brother followed us, and he told my father. I was so afraid to go home because I knew that I was going to get into trouble. I was put on punishment for it, and I was told never to see the boy again. I was so upset that I cried, and I was sent to my room. I had to be on punishment in my room, and for some reason, I hated that place. I spent most of my time there. I was never allowed to go out. Yes, I did things, such as sneak places I knew I was not suppose to be; but when I could be trusted and had no intention of doing anything; I just kept on being accused of everything. I was so mad about this. My heart was good and I knew this, but why couldn't anyone see it?

I continued to keep sneaking with this boy, and my daddy would keep coming to get me when my stepmother did not. My stepmother would always let my daddy deal with me. Because, I think deep down inside she knew that she was really causing it, and she was afraid it would come out. Even when I stayed after school, I would get into trouble. I loved to run track and play field hockey; these are the sports that I played when I was in high school. When I was in the 7th grade, I was running outdoor track with the senior high girls. I ran anchor for the 4x4 relay team as a 7th grader. I was the fastest girl in my grade. I ran a lot with the boys and this is why I was so fast. I did really well in field hockey until I was hit in face just below my right eye. I never really wanted to play after that. I was always told by my coach that I could run track in college on a scholarship if I applied myself to my work. I was just so hurt and confused by everything that was going on at home that I could not seem to concentrate on school. I could not get myself to see what everyone else saw in me. I was the fastest girl in the district on the track team and no one could beat me in anything that I participated in. My coach would push me so much to my maximum potential and she would ask me on several occasions if something was wrong and if there was anything bothering me? I would tell her no because I did not want anyone to repeat anything I said to anyone. How could I explain all of the bad things that were going on at home? The things that I had to talk about were not even normal. I just decided to keep the issues to myself and deal with things on my own. I realized that all of the issues were destroying my life but I could not afford to share them with anyone.

CHAPTER 19

My Life Had Changed...I Was Miserable

My life had changed so much for the worse. God, was nowhere on the scene. I was miserable, hurt, and confused all of the time. I was young, I had to learn how to smile, and just get through it. Many people out there were probably mistaking all of what I was doing for puberty and being young, but that was not the case at all. I was abused and hurt at a very young age, and I was trying very hard to deal with that without opening my mouth and telling somebody about it.

My stepmother had orchestrated ways of making me look like I was crazy, so who was going to believe me anyway? I did not ask to come here in this world and be treated like this. I did not deserve this. Daddy, where are you, *God*, where are you? Why don't you help me? How could I love a stepmother who tried to make me stop loving my daddy? Then she even tried to make me stop loving God, who is my Heavenly Father? As a young girl, this was very hard to believe, as well as understand. It says in the bible in several scriptures, that *God will never leave you nor forsake you* and that *He is a loving and just God*. I could not feel this at all. Could it be that when my stepmother told me that I could not go to church anymore, that I began to think in my own mind as a child that God was bad? Children are taught at a young age by their parents or someone who is raising them what they are supposed to do in life. Whatever they are being taught, whether it be right or wrong; they are going to learn it. I remember someone saying to me one time, "What you live, you learn."

I loved my daddy, because I just did. I do not know why. He never abused me, and he treated me fairly. He gave me kisses and hugs when I came to him for them. He brought me nice things when I needed it, he just did not protect me very well and he always sided with whatever my stepmother told him. This was very hard for me to understand, because I remember watching other girls daddy's protect and take care of them, and I wanted this too. I felt as if I was so misunderstood, and I was only responding to one thing "abuse." The only reason why I acted the way I did at this time in my life was because I was abused by my stepmother. And it was being repeated throughout my life. Sure, I ran track and played field hockey, lived in a nice house and everyone thought what they were looking at was the way it was for real but I could never get out of my head my abuse and what was going on at home when I was doing it. I had to go back to the abuse and the silence and deal with the things that were happening with no one there to help me through the pain and hurt.

I hated to go home. There were times when I would stay away from home all day just so I did not have to go home and deal with my stepmother. I knew there was a world out there for me to see, and there were dreams and ambitions in that I wanted to fulfill, but I could not get them done because of her. I felt like she was jealous of me, and she had nothing I wanted. My daddy was my daddy before he was her husband, and that was by no fault of mine. I did not ask to come here, and I did not ask for the life that was being given to me. I was innocent. I was a child. All I wanted was to love my daddy, and I could have loved her too, but she would not let me. I remember a time when she took me clothes shopping, and she wanted me to pick out the clothes *she* wanted and because I did not like the clothes she liked she got mad. I was different from her, and I did not like her style or taste of clothes. I was not her biological daughter, and I did not have the dreams and ambitions that she had either. Was that so wrong? Was that so bad? I just wanted what I wanted, and I was not going to settle for the things that she wanted for me. I was not angry, but I did want to be able to make me own choices sometimes. I wanted to be the person that God made me to be, whoever that was? I was not spiteful or deceitful to get my way I just wanted what I wanted sometimes. I have always been different, and I always dared to be different no matter what it cost me. You know it's like when Jesus realized the price he was going to have to pay for dying on the cross; He decided to do it anyway. The bible says *He was in the garden of Gethsemane praying until He began to sweat what looked like beads of sweat and blood because he was travailing so much in His prayers to His Father about His Father God saying to God, let the cup pass from me! There was no other way to do it. Jesus knew He had to do it.* Somewhere, deep down inside even as a child I knew there was something very deep spiritually that God wanted me to do. The more I tried to do right the more my stepmother would try to force me to do things the way she wanted me to do them. I believe the time I was in that Apostolic-Pentecostal church that something happened to me to make me always want to do what I knew was right to do no matter what. People were my biggest challenge. It seemed like most of the challenging me where the people in my own family. My father even started to seem like he was not happy with my stepmother anymore, and he would have talks with me about it sometimes. I remember one time he gave me his wedding ring that my stepmother had given him. He told me I could have it. I remember putting it on a chain and wearing it around my neck and she saw me with it, and she took it from me. Then she asked me where I got it. I told her my father gave it to me. I never heard anything else about it again but even as a child I knew that was very strange and something was very wrong. I was only a young girl and what would make a daddy do this?

CHAPTER 20

My Stepmother was Not a Talker

My father had a job where he was never home. He was a truck driver, and he would sometimes be on the road for days at a time. While he was away is when my stepmother would just constantly pick at me, or she would just treat me as if I was not even there. I would do the same thing and not talk to her because I would not want to say anything to her that would make her angry. I was just too young for all of this. She made me do laundry, cook and clean, but she would never teach me girl things or show me any love. Like how to dress up and what to look for in a man when I grew up, or what college should I attend? I even remember sucking my thumb and my teeth getting crooked; and when I went to my daddy to ask for braces, I never got them. My daddy had good insurance, but I could not get braces. I was very conscious of my teeth, because I enjoyed smiling, but I did not like having crooked teeth. It never really stopped me from getting the things I wanted, but I did want to look pretty. I was not asking for much just could I have a pretty smile. The things that I wanted from them never seemed to be what I got but where was all of the abuse coming from? How is it that the things that I knew were right and I knew how I should have been treated but it seemed so hard for them to give me? I would just ask them for things that were normal things that any child would ask their parents for. My stepmother and my father never talked. They were in the house, and the house was beautiful and spotless, but it was not a home filled with love.

On the weekends, my brothers and daddy would be cutting the grass and I would be inside cleaning the house with my stepmother. I had to clean the whole house, while my brothers would cut the grass. I just always felt so bothered by being around my stepmother. My father and brothers would all be working together and laughing with each other, and on the inside of the house my stepmother and I would be in total silence. I wanted so much to go outside and be with them having fun talking and laughing. I could not understand what could have happened in her life to make her treat me this way?

CHAPTER 21

My Grandmother...My Stepmother's Mother

My grandmother, who was my stepmother's mother seemed so nice and kind. She was a church-going woman who went to church every Sunday. She would tell us about God, and sometimes we would go to church with her. But I did not like the church she went to, because I did not feel what I felt in my grandmother's church what I felt in Highway Gospel. That church believed in the baptism, the Holy Ghost, and speaking in tongues. My grandmother's church did not speak in tongues or receive the Holy Ghost.

I loved spending the night at her house so I could have time to get away from my stepmother, and have a chance to have some peace. My grandmother was nice to me, and she would bake and cook food. I would walk to the store and buy things, and sit and talk to her about God. I never heard her cuss, and no one would ever cuss around her. She was quiet, but she was a Godly woman, and everyone in the family knew it. She lived in Coatesville in a little apartment not far from town. She moved from the country when I was younger because my stepmother thought she might be getting too old to stay by herself. Where she lived in the country there were no other house around her for miles. I would always stay at her house and never wanted to go home. When I was growing up I remember her just being a saved Christian woman who always went to church. She passed away when I was about 16 years old. My cousin went to stay with her to help her because my stepmother's side of the family thought it might be nice for someone to be there and help her. One day the phone rang early in the morning and all I remember my stepmother doing was leaving the house and crying. She drove to my grandmother's house by herself and when she got there the ambulance and paramedics were there trying to revive here. She had died in her sleep. My stepmother came back home and just cried. I was upset too because I loved my grandmother. I remember them having a funeral service for her and all of our family on my stepmother's side being there. It was a sad day for me, but it did not hurt me like it did when my other grandmother died. I only hurt for a little while when my stepmother's mother died. The one good thing about her dying was that she did not experience any pain. She just went off to sleep and never woke up. I wonder if her being so close to God made her go this way?

CHAPTER 22

My Older Brother Gets Abused

My stepmother and my younger brother had a very close relationship with each other. I was very close to him because we were very close in age, and we played with each other every day. My stepmother would cater to him, and she would do things for my older brother because he would accept everything she did, no matter what even if it was wrong.

I remember clearly one time when we were all in the house together my parents were at work; my older brother who was about 13 years old at the time and my younger brother were wrestling on the floor in the living room. My younger brother kept jumping on my older brothers back and scratching him because his nails stayed really long when he was younger. My older brother kept telling him to stop because he was finished playing and his nails were making him bleed, but my younger brother would not stop. They started yelling at each other. After a while my younger brother got angry and started hitting my older brother. My older brother was doing everything he could to get him off of him, but he just kept on hitting him and scratching him. That is when a knock came on the front door where we were at. My older brother asked, "Who is it?" It was my stepmother on the front porch because I could see her when I looked out the curtains. She would not answer my brother. I told my older brother who it was and he opened the door. After my older brother opened the door, she just started beating on him and saying to him, "You better keep your hands off of my baby." My older brother was trying to explain what had happened but she would not listen to him. She just kept on beating him until he ran out into the front yard with nothing but his underwear on, in broad day light. In addition, she had a wooden bat in her hand, and hit him in the head with it. I remember my older brother grabbing his head, and I was just standing there crying because I knew the whole time what had happened. But I was afraid for myself being hit. When she asked me what happened I just told her the truth. But, I remained calm while telling her. I was so afraid that day, and I could not believe what she had done to my older brother. I knew I even took a chance telling here what really happened that day but I could not lie to here. I had to do what I knew was right. My daddy always instilled in us to tell the truth and this is what I was going to do.

My older brother was one of the nicest people anyone could ever meet. He had a great personality, and he was a relatively happy kid. He was the one in the family who had very fair skin, and sandy-brown hair. My daddy had silky jet-black hair that he wore in an afro, and my younger brother and I favored him. My older brother did not look like either one of my parents. I often wondered why he looked this way, but he was my brother and I loved him. We were really close when we were real little in foster care, but when we came home to live with my daddy we drifted apart from each other. I remember him being very distant from everyone in the family. And as he grew older, he would mostly play with the white kids and hang out with them all of the time.

Where we lived was predominately white people. My cousins were the only blacks in the neighborhood and he hardly ever played over there. He wrestled in school, ran track, and played football, just as my younger brother did. He was very shy when he was younger. When he got older, he went on to become the President of the Student Council and won the most Popular Person in his class award. He also was a Chippendale male stripper too. I remember watching the television one time and the phone rang. It was one of my relatives letting me know to turn on *Good Morning America,* which was a famous television show because my older brother was dancing on there. I turned the channel and there he was. No one ever thought this would happen because of his shyness as a child. He really began to blossom as he got older. The one thing that always puzzled me is how he would always make people believe that he was not black but he was white. He would tell everyone that he was adopted and that we were not his real family. I was the one who felt the strongest about this because he was my biological brother and not my stepbrother. He did not acknowledge me as his real sister and that hurt me too. I did not care what he said, he was still my brother and I loved him as he was.

As we got older, we started to see less and less of each other. My older brother was allowed to go to dances at school, and stay overnight at his friend's house. He would leave almost every weekend to go off with his friends. I wanted him to know everything that was going on while he was not there, but I was afraid to tell him because of fear that he would run back and repeat it to my stepmother. My brother somehow was able to get love her in a way that was not healthy. He knew he was being mistreated by her, but he loved her in spite of what she did. It was as if he was letting her know that no matter what she did to him, he adored her anyway. I did not feel this way at all. I was not trying to be mean to her, but I did want to let her know that I did not like being abused or mistreated, and that everything she did to me hurt me. I did not have a happy life, but somehow my brother learned to mask and deal with it. I do not care whatever she did to him he always looked at it like it was normal behavior. How is it normal getting hit in the head with a wooden bat and getting beat outside in the broad daylight with nothing but your underwear on? This is not normal behavior at all. He did not even do anything that was that bad to deserve what he got that day.

CHAPTER 23

Daddies are Special to their Daughters

I felt all of the abuse from the time it started until that day as if it had just happened to me. I wanted so desperately to have a life of happiness but I wanted to know why I was being abused and was I doing things that were so wrong that it just kept on happening to me?

I was a kid, a young girl loving her daddy, and wanting so desperately to be loved back. Why couldn't you love me back Daddy? Why couldn't you protect me? Were you so busy living your own life that you couldn't even see what was happening to your children, your baby girl? I was your baby girl. I was Daddy's girl and I didn't even know why. I loved my daddy with a love that I couldn't even explain. No matter how much he didn't protect me or love me the way I needed to be loved, I loved him. He was my hero. Daddys are special to their daughters, and they are the first man that any daughter will ever see before they start dating and become women and growing up and marrying that special man in their life; their husband. Fathers need to know that this is a very special time in any daughter's life to have that time with their daddy(s) to share things with and buy them things. Go out to dinner, and even the movies. I never got to do any of these things with my daddy by myself. I missed all of it because of my stepmother, someone he chose to bring into his life to love and marry. She was the one who separated me from my daddy and having a real relationship with me. Daddy you should have never gone to get me in the foster home. I did not ask you to come get me. I did not even know you. Daddy how could you let this happen? I didn't even know that I was beautiful and as gorgeous as people said until they told me. I should have been told this by you. My father was keeping me hidden and telling me not to date boys, but he never told me why. I wanted to talk to him about why my stepmother abused me when I was seven, but he would always become hostile when I brought it up. He would always say that my stepmother loved me, and she would never do anything to hurt me. But that was not true, and I knew he knew it. All of the pain and hurt and not being able to talk to my daddy about. This was causing me to drift even further away from doing what I knew was right. The reason why I wanted so desperately to do right was because I wanted God to be pleased with me and I wanted my life to be right. I wanted to stay a virgin until I was married because I had been taught this by Pastor Lucado and his ministry. Even though I only had a brief period with Pastor Lucado and his church, a lot was planted in me. The bible says, in 1 Corinthians 3:6, *"One plants, another waters, and God gives the increase."* God already knew that this would happen. He knew that I was in a family that would not let me go to church and worship and praise Him but the seed of holiness was still planted in me. The Apostolic-Pentecostal seed was planted in me and it fell on fertile ground the day I found Christ in their ministry and I did enough of what I was allowed to do for it to take root in me and be birthed. Because the bible says, in *Exodus 20:12 "Children obey your parents and your days will be long upon this earth."*

This is the reason why I did not dare go behind my parents backs and continue to keep doing things that pertained to God in their house. They were not happy with me worshipping with Pastor Lucado and they made that very clear to me. I just stopped to keep the peace and to be obedient and not make things worse.

CHAPTER 24

Pastor Lucado and His Family

Pastor Lucado's family was amazing. He had a daughter named Roe that had a laugh that was so funny. No one could laugh like her. I adored her. She taught me how to wear my skirts long and my blouses up high enough to cover my chest to look presentable in the ministry. Back then, she would make her jean skirts out of old jeans.

Bruce her brother is the key reason how I got started in the ministry. Because if he had not of come up to me on the steps of the courthouse in West Chester the day of the parade so many years before I would have never gotten to know his father or even went to their church.

As a child, I yearned to go back to church and have the experiences that I had while being in church with them. I remember sitting on the front row with other girls, separated from the boys. Being watched by church mothers who would hit us over the hands and make us sit still. I remember getting on the alter to tarry for the Holy Ghost, and having to stay there until I got it. I would be crying and saying, "I'm tire!", but they would make me stay there anyway. I was so young, but I loved everything about the ministry and God. I remember riding to church in their blue van and all of us would be packed in there. We would be laughing and having a lot of fun until I had to go home. The joy I had with them was not happening in my house. It was the total opposite. No one would be laughing. I would come home and just be walking on pins and needles, knowing that if I did one wrong thing I could get hit or punished.

CHAPTER 25

Living Day to Day with a Monster...My Stepmother

Living with my stepmother was like living day to day with a Doctor Jekel and Mr. Hyde. You never knew what to expect from her but you knew that one of them was there, and able to hurt you whenever they wanted to. She would show everyone this nice person when she was outside the house or if someone would come visit but when it was just me and her she was mean and cruel. I even tried to get my family to come to church with me but they would not go. They did not want anything to do with it. I remember thinking to myself, was I ever going to get out of this mess that I was born into? All of the picnics, vacations, movies, and dinner that I went on, but no one knew the pain I felt inside. I was hurting so bad and there was no one there that understood me or anyone who tried to help me. I can remember so clearly trying so hard to stay nice in the mist of all the bad things that were going on with me.

I felt so misunderstood. Why did everyone think that I was this girl that wanted to be abused and mistreated all the time and I wasn't? Why did it seem like everyone was trying to change me and make me what they wanted me to be? I was a good girl, and that is what I was trying so much to hang on to. Where was God? Daddy where are you? And why did they both keep on letting these bad things happen to me. I can remember a time in my life when a letter came in the mail addressed to me. I never received any mail from anyone and I was shocked when my daddy told me that I had a letter sent to me. I had just come in the door from track practice and he said there is a letter for you. Right away, a feeling came over me that something was not right. I felt something strange in the pit of my stomach. I remember looking at my stepmother and thinking I know she has got something to do with this. She was not saying a word. I looked at the envelope and I thought to myself, why is the handwriting so bad and ugly. I knew my stepmother had written it to me. I just knew it. I was about 16 and who could have wrote this letter to me with such ugly handwriting? Something said to me, "Your stepmother did it, but she used her other hand to write it with." She could write with both hands, and I forget what they call these types of people? I opened the letter and began to read it. I was sickened at what I read. The first sentence said, "Now that you have gotten your cherry popped everyone is going to talk about you, and think of you as being dirty and filthy." I could not remember the whole letter, but this is the one thing that stood out in my mind. I knew she did it because back then we did not even use those types of words. I just remember crying and my daddy asking me what was wrong? I showed the letter to him and as he was reading it he said, "Who could have wrote all of this filthy stuff?" I said, "I know who did it." He said, "Who?" Then I said, "If I tell you, you're not going to believe me." He said, "Monday I am going to take you down to the school and meet with your principal about this, because whoever wrote this is sick and I want to know who did this!" I looked at my stepmother, and she was not even responding to any of it. My father said, "Honey, look at this." While she was skimming over the letter, she did not even have any reaction to the letter, she just gave it back to my daddy so he could keep it until Monday morning when he took me to school to meet with the principal about the letter. I remember Monday morning coming and the principal calling me into his office to meet with him first before my father got a chance to speak to him. He asked me who I thought could have done such a thing to me? I said, "I know who did it and it is my stepmother who did it." He was shocked and he said to me, "Michele, do you have any idea why she would of done this to you." I said, "Yes, she did it because she doesn't like me too much and she has been doing things to me since I was 7 years old." He then told me to go out in the lobby and have a seat until he met with my father. He told my father what I said and when my father came out of the office the principal call us both in so I could tell him what I said. When I started to say who I thought wrote the letter my father started saying, "No, Michele your mother did not do this and why do you always try to create problems in my house?" I just shut up at that point because I knew I was not going to get him to believe me. He took me home and we never discussed that letter again.

I went on back to school the next day and I just sat in every class and did nothing. I did not care what happened to me after that. I ended up failing every class that semester and I did not care one bit. When we finally got our report cards, my stepmother saw my report card, and told me Michele you will not be put on punishment this time because of all of the pressure you are under. I just remember looking at her and thinking to myself, "I wonder who was the cause of it all?"

I was able to do just about whatever I wanted as far as a 16 year old is concerned, I could talk on the phone to my friends, go outside and hang with my cousins and other kids in the neighborhood. I was a tom-boy, so I hung out with my brothers and their friends. I had a lot of fun but I still was not satisfied with the way I was being treated and made to accept the behavior that was directed towards me. I knew it wasn't me and it was not my fault but why was I being made to look like the culprit? Nothing was going right in school or at home. I was running outdoor track that year like I always did and I loved it but I was not even excelling in that either. I needed someone to help me through this before I end up making choices in life that I will regret. All of my dreams and talents were crumbling right in front of me and I could not even do anything about it.

CHAPTER 26

Feeling as if No One Loves or Cares Anything about Me

I am 17 years old, and I'm feeling as if no one loves or cares anything about me. My brothers were gone most of the time, and I was always ending up at home with my stepmother having to do chores and being on punishment all the time.

For months at a time, we would be walking around the house in complete and total silence to each other. The only time she talked to me was when my father came home. I do not see how my father did not know, and if he did, why wasn't he there for me? Daddies are supposed to protect their children, not let harm come to them. I was his real daughter, not his stepdaughter. If he wasn't going to treat me right, why did he ever come get me and my older brother from out of foster care? He should have just left us both there; we might have been better off. At times I wondered what my life would have been like had he of done this? Why did he have to go and mess it all up for my brother and me? I hated being here and living with parents who care more about themselves, than us.

I remember praying to God for Him to help me get the life that I wanted and needed so badly. I wanted friends and a future someday. I wanted a life of peace, and happiness but it just seemed like it was not going to ever happen. I spent most of my time alone with no one to talk to. There was one person who I did talk to when I could. I would go to her house, and we would talk. I found out her father used to date my biological mother when they were younger. Her name was, Rhonda Pearson. She was a true friend to me, and I really liked her. We got along great and I could tell her anything and she would keep it to herself. She knew all of what I was going through. She would always tell me to come to her house whenever I wanted or and to call her and talk whenever I needed to. I would never call her on the phone because of my stepmother always trying to listen in on the phone conversations and never respecting my privacy. I know parents should always know what their children are doing and no child should ever really think that they have total privacy but my stepmother was never given a reason to not trust me. I was a good girl and she never tried to figure that out. My girlfriend's brother began to like me once I started to get closer to her. He wanted me to be his girlfriend, and we were together for a brief period of time but I just did not like him, and I did not want to be with him. One reason is that I still liked Bruce Lucado, even though he was busy doing other things and dating other girls. I tried to get Paul to come over my house one time so he could be the one to take my virginity. I was still a virgin and I wanted to stay this way until I was married but I was feeling so lost and alone from all that I was going through. Everything that I wanted so bad to do right just seemed like it was all in vain. I was never allowed to go to any of my proms or any dances. I was not allowed to hang out with my friends or date. I had to sneak to go to Rhonda's house. Imagine going all the way through high school and never going to one prom. All of my dreams were fading everyday from me. I just did not care anymore. If I was going to lose my virginity, I wanted it to be with Bruce Lucado. I had liked him ever since we were in second grade. He agreed to it too. One day on his birthday, he decided to come to my house after school. We got off the bus at my bus stop, and we started to walk to my house together. I was so nervous walking to my house and deep down inside I did not really want to do it but no one cared about me trying to remain a virgin until I was married. All of my friends had already lost their virginity to someone. Why should I save myself for my husband now? If I was going to do it, it may as well be with someone I love. Bruce waited at the top of my driveway, until I went and saw who was home. My older brother was home that day.

I remember coming back out to tell him but he had l already left. I was upset, but I really believe that God did not want that for me. We remained friends until I was in 11th grade. My brother was not even supposed to be home that day. How is it that he was. God has a strange way of doing things. My only question is why did he do things this way?

Bruce was a senior and he really did not pay me any attention. I was going through so much, and I was never allowed to date him because my father did not like him. Why couldn't they just trust me? I wanted to do the right thing, and I would have done it if they would have trusted me. Bruce and I never really talked about what happened that day and why he left but I just knew God intervened that day because He really did not want me to lose my virginity this way. I wondered was I attractive and did I look beautiful to him? I was always told by a lot of different boys that I was the best looking girl in school. Why could I not see it?

CHAPTER 27

My Diary

I was about 17 years old now, and my feelings were getting even more numb. I had a diary that I wrote in everyday, and I would hide it under my mattress. I didn't have anyone to talk to now since the only friend I had was gone. She moved away from me and went back to school in West Chester. One day I could tell that someone got into my diary and was reading it. I felt so betrayed and violated that I demanded to know who read it, but no one would admit it. I remember going to my younger brother and asking him if he had read it, and he said, "No!" Then I went to my older brother and asked him and he also said, "No!" My stepmother was doing laundry, and I remember asking her because my sheets were taken off my bed and she was hanging them on the line, and I remember saying to her, "Why did you take my diary and read it?" She said, "I did not take your stinking diary!" I was crying and upset; I could not understand why she did this to me. I already knew she was the one who did it, but I thought I would ask my brothers first just to be sure I was not just accusing her of something she did not do.

My father came home from work shortly after that and I was crying while trying to tell my father what she had done, but he said to me, "Michele, don't you start, I know your mother did not do this." I could not believe it; I was at my wits end by now, being accused of things that I was not doing. I was totally all out of feelings by this time. This was just all too much for me. I had too many hurts and let downs that I could not take anymore. Looking back at all of the things that she had done to me I could not even count how many times she had hurt me and devastated me with things that meant a lot to me. I did not love myself. How could I love myself when I had never been showed any real love, only by my grandmother and now she was gone. Why did she leave me here to go through all of this hurt and pain by myself? There were so many things that my stepmother had done to me. I knew at this point that I had to leave. I could not take any more of this.

My stepmother even took a pair of sneakers that my daddy's sister brought me and cut the sneakers up on the sides and then put them back where she found them as if nothing even happened right after my diary was taken. Then I had to call my daddy's sister up on the phone to tell her what had happened so she could buy me another pair. She acted as if she did not even believe me. I could not believe the way I was being treated, and I was being made to look like the bad person I was not.

I knew things were not going to work. Therefore, I wanted to leave my parents house because I did not want to get blamed for breaking up their marriage, like my daddy would always say; and I did not want to continue to be treated like a stepchild; which is what all of this felt like to me. I could not stay in this house another day. I was going through so much, and no one was listening to me. I was not getting any love from anyone, and I did not ask to come here. I started asking questions like, why was I born to go through all of this? Why did God allow my stepmother whom my daddy married to do all of this to me? I then started thinking he was so selfish. All he cared about was what he wanted, he did not care about me.

Everyone I liked, she hated; and everything I wanted to do she crushed, including all of my dreams and plans that I had. She even took God away from me. What parents wouldn't want their child to serve God. I loved God, and I wanted so desperately to serve Him. However, doesn't the bible say in Exodus 20:12, *"To honor your Father and your Mother and your days will be long upon this earth?"* Therefore, I had to honor them because I knew what the word said. I was going through so much and did not know what to do. I do not even remember acknowledging God in any of this because of how my stepmother told me not to worship Him.

I was in an Apostolic-Pentecostal Church, and they worshipped God in the fullness of the bible. They believed in laying on of hands, casting out demons in Jesus' name, speaking in other tongues, and being baptized and filled with the Holy Ghost. I could not explain why God was not there for me? The bible says in Hebrews 13:5, *"He'll never leave me nor forsake me,"* but where was He at? Where was my earthly Daddy at? I was a girl who many people thought had it all. I lived in a nice house in an all-white neighborhood in the country. I dressed nice every day. My parents drove nice cars, we got plenty to eat, and the lights and phone were never turned off, but I was living a life of hurt and pain. I was smiling trying to cover it up. I tried so desperately to please both of my parents but it never worked. The only time my stepmother was pleased with me was when I bought her something. This made her happy, so I always found myself bringing her things just to keep a smile on her face. She still would not talk to me or deal with me though. I remember telling the school guidance counselor how my stepmother would treat me because I could not anymore of the abuse and the people came to my house and when the woman left my father said to me, "Michele, there must be something wrong with you because all you keep doing is causing trouble for everyone." I was so hurt by this statement coming from my daddy who never tried to once protect me from his wife or try to even make sure I was okay. I almost felt like I hated him for saying this. My daddy meant the world to me because he was my real daddy and I had an attachment to him that I could not even understand. I was put on punishment most of the time, especially after that Children and Youth Service woman left our house that day. I did not lie about anything I said. I remember my daddy always making us tell the truth no matter what but he was not being truthful at all that day when he lied and told the woman from CYS that I made up all of the stuff that was being said. I lost a lot of respect for my daddy that day for not telling the truth when he was asked if my stepmother and I had a good relationship and did she ever punish me in ways that were in appropriate? I knew I was going to get in trouble but it did not even matter to me. My parents even had my brothers convinced that I was making all of it up. God knew I was not making it up but let's not bring Him into the picture because He knew all of this was happening to me and He never came to my rescue one time. This only made me not want to serve Him at all. I thought God was love and protected everyone. Why was I not being protected? My earthly father would not protect me so why should God protect me? How can God protect me anyway when he does not even have hands to protect me? My father must have had something bad happen to him as a child and maybe this is why he could not protect me. He never really talked to me so how was I supposed to know what was going on with him. Maybe I would have understood if he would have talked to me about his childhood and how he was raised. This could not be the case because my brothers did not experience what I went through. I had my mind made up I was going to leave. That day I went to my stepmother and told her I was going to leave her house. She agreed to let me go but she told me she wanted me to leave before my father got home. She took me to Coatesville at my Aunt's house and dropped me off. That was where I experienced what I thought was going to be the best times of my life but it turned out to be even more pain and devastation.

CHAPTER 28

The Final Chapter

I want everybody to know that me deciding to write this book was not meant to hurt or expose anyone, I just want everyone to know that the things that happened to me were very real and a lot of other girls and boys just like me are going through things like this. Many are going through rejection, molestation, rape, and abuse that is verbal and physical. No child deserves to experience any kind of pain or devastation like this. The one point I am trying to make is that parents should be more mindful whenever they decide to accept someone else's children as their own. The world is made up of over 90% blended families and I wonder how many of the children in those homes have experienced: rejection, molestation, rape, and abuse? Parents want to be together but how many of them really ever stop and think about the child or children that will be involved in the situation? I believe everybody has some kind of idea how they feel about that child or children before they decide to commit to the person who they belong to biologically. Sometimes you might just have to walk away if it means bringing harm to the child or children that do not deserve it. Children are people too and will one day grow up after they have been wrongly treated and become adults. Just think how many children are out here in this world that have experienced abuse from a family member or babysitter that a parent thinks they can trust? Children will not tell the truth because most of them have been threatened not to tell. The hurts of an innocent child will one day come out and when it does the world will have to reap more: rejection, molestation, rape, and abuse, sometimes even murder. I thank God that I never had the kind of heart to ever want to harm or murder my stepmother for all that she had done to me. I pray that this book will bless every reader that reads it and that everyone from a child to an adult will think about what they have read and be mindful of what they are going through and even if it is an adult or parent they will be mindful of who they are going to attach themselves to, as far as relationships are concerned. Always ask yourself if you feel as though the person is right for you and if you can be a good example of a parent to the child or children in that relationship. You will be the person to lead and guide that child into their future. Even if the relationship is only for a short period make sure you make every minute count. Make sure you are a positive role model to that child or children's life. I will admit that things might not be easy for you but just think how a child is going to feel not knowing you or maybe not even wanting you there in their parent's life or their life. Being an adult is not easy but you must try real hard to be patient and remember love suffers long and does not give up or want what is best for itself. Love is patient and kind and learns to understand that even if I as a child says something that may make you upset or maybe even do something that might make you want to lose your temper; just remember I am nothing but a child who needs you to understand that I need to be protected and loved so I can grow up to be the person that God intended for me to be. As far as biological parents are concerned I encourage you to be mindful of the people you allow to come into your child or children's lives and not to allow them to experience the devastating things that can happen to them. Pay more attention to where you send them and make it your sole responsibility to always take the time to listen to what they are saying to you. No child will just make up things just to be making them up. Daddy's love your daughters and protect them with your life. I know some daddy's might have sons but daddy and daughter relationships are special and the daughters will one day grow up and go out and look for someone just like you to marry and have children with someday. Daddy's teach your son or sons how to be respectful and not to spread themselves around with every girl or woman they meet. Parents are supposed to teach their children about integrity and God. I am older now and have had many things happen to me even after I left home and I was able to go out on my own and have children. God blessed me with 5 beautiful children. Three are adults now and are experiencing the same things that I had to face because of watching me go through hurts and devastation's trying to work through problems that they were born into. It took me years to work through my problems with my stepmother and be able to stand and be the woman that God has destined me to be. I was about 30 years old when I finally let go of the pain and heartache she caused me. My purpose was to write this book to enlighten everyone of the importance of the message that is inside of it. I had to go through all of this pain and tragedy so someone else could be healed. Be healed!! This book is just a small glimpse of my childhood but two more books will follow this one that will go into even more devastation and heartache as I take my journey into a world that has always been sheltered from me as a child. As I go into adulthood, I will leave the country and go live in the city into one of the worst times anyone can ever imagine. My next book is entitled: *Daddy, Why Won't You Come!!* Look for it soon.

May God Bless all the children in Jesus' Name.

ABOUT THE AUTHOR
Michele Sweeney

Michele Sweeney was born and raised in Downingtown, Pennsylvania; and lived there until the age of seventeen and now resides in the City of Coatesville, Pennsylvania. She is the mother of five beautiful children and seven grandchildren. Michele has had many jobs working with juvenile delinquents, and she has also worked with other children. Children are very special to her, and she finds great joy in helping and mentoring them to become better people. She attended Downingtown High until 12th grade in which she did not graduate due to all of the problems she was having at home. Things were so overwhelming for her that she decided to drop out. After the drop out, she decided to return to school with her father in which they both received their GED's together in 1989.

Michele received her Computer Specialist degree in 1992. She has also gone on to pursue an Associates of Arts degree in Criminal Justice and is now working very hard on her Bachelor's Degree in Criminal Justice, in which she will graduate March 2013. She has also received training and is Sex Offender certified. Michele plans to one day pursue a career in law enforcement. She is also very active in her church where she is a powerful prayer warrior and intercessor. The church that she attends is A. D. Baxter Memorial Church of God in Christ, located in Coatesville, PA, under the leadership of her Pastors; Pastor Montez O. Jones and Pastor Alfonso B. Baxter. Sr. She finds great joy and peace in this ministry. She just recently made this transition from a ministry called, "Brighter Way Ministries located in Newark, DE, where she served under the leadership of Pastor Clarence "Ernie" Stevens and First Lady Anne Stevens.

Michele served as a Deaconess at this church and also as an Armor Bearer for her Pastor and First Lady. Writing this book, Michele had no idea what God had planned for her. She was just trying to be obedient to God one day when He spoke to her through a family member who knows her from a child, to write this book. She had no idea that a book would unfold to this degree to change the lives of men, women, and children especially. Even though we might have to go through something that is so painful and humiliating at that time can in the end, after we have gone through the "Fire of affliction; can bring us out like pure gold!" If you struggle with the pain of your past and being a child of rejection and disappointment after being born and not being the blame for anything that has happened to you by means of: rejection, betrayal, abuse, rape, molestation, lies, or deception; this book is for you. May you read it, and be blessed abundantly in Jesus Name. THIS WAS TRULY A GOD THING!!!

www.ingramcontent.com/pod-product-compliance
Lightning Source LLC
Chambersburg PA
CBHW051455290426
44109CB00016B/1768